VISUAL EDITION · GREAT WORKS COLLECTION

Santiago Cathedral

PHOTOGRAPHS: CARLOS GIORDANO RODRÍGUEZ AND NICOLÁS PALMISANO SOSA

DOSDEPUBLISHING   VISUAL GUIDES GREAT WORKS

01

02

05

CONTENTS

**Capital of the
Glory Portico**

01

A SYMBOL OF CHRISTIANITY

The genesis of the cathedral

Construction work started on the Cathedral of Santiago de Compostela in 1075 to protect the apostle's relics.

In the eighth century most of the Iberian Peninsula was under Muslim rule, which, through conquests and treaties with Visigoth rulers, had woven a web of influence that went beyond the Pyrenees. The Christian pockets of resistance against the invader were concentrated in the north of Spain, where the Kingdom of Asturias began a land annexation process that allowed it to extend its borders to the east and the west. Moreover, religion provided a symbolic meaning to this reconquest policy of the Asturian monarchs, who contributed to the development of an episcopal network. In the ninth century, from the bishopric of Iria Flavia (close to present day Santiago de Compostela) came the news of the discovery of a mausoleum that held the remains of James the Greater, one of Jesus Christ's apostles. A church was built to protect his relics, quickly replaced by a larger one that was able to respond to the early pilgrimages and underpin the cohesion of the territory. However, the increasing enthusiasm for the Jacobean cult meant the design of the temple had to correspond with the importance of the relics, and by 1075 construction work began on Santiago Cathedral, an edifice that was inseparable from its surrounding urban structure and the infrastructures that connected the Iberian Peninsula to the rest of Europe.

Apostle Saint James the Greater
Christ's disciple depicted as a pilgrim —with the staff and pumpkin— presides over the high altar.

Decoration of the high altar
The temple's main chapel is the most important example of Baroque art inside the cathedral.

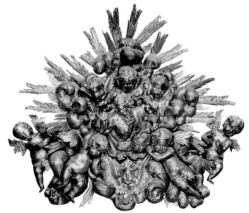

The story of Saint James

The initiative of a temple dedicated to James the Greater is based on the tradition that situates the apostle's tomb at the far north-west end of the Iberian Peninsula.

◐ **Window**
Made from granite it belongs to the reconstruction that was carried out in the 10th century of the basilica built by Alfonso III, damaged in an attack by Muslim troops.

A special disciple

According to the *New Testament*, James the Greater (or *Santiago* as he is known in Spanish), along with his brother, John the Evangelist, became one of Christ's first apostles after giving up his work as a fisherman in Galilee. Known as the *Son of Thunder* for his strong character, he was one of Christ's favourite disciples and appears in crucial passages of the Gospels such as that of the prayer in the *Garden of Olives*, which narrates the moments prior to Jesus' capture. The Bible also describes his death in Jerusalem in the year 44AD by order of Herod Agrippa, who persecuted the Christians to curry favour with the Jews. According to various sources, Saint James' body was moved by two of his disciples from Jaffa, Israel to the Iberian Peninsula, where the apostle had supposedly preached after Christ's death, in order to be buried.

◐ **Goodyear altar**
A gift to Santiago Cathedral in the year 1456, it has five alabaster panels that narrate scenes from the apostle's life.

Bishop Theodemar
He found the relics of James after being alerted by a hermit who had seen lights over the tomb.

20
METRES
is the supposed length of the first church built dedicated to the apostle James the Greater.

1 The conversion
Jesus finds James fishing on Lake Tiberias (Sea of Galilee).

HISTORY

A period of change

The discovery of the sepulchre is set in a period of territorial tension in the Iberian Peninsula, marked by invasions and the birth of new kingdoms.

Kingdom of Asturias

Umayyad Caliphate

720
IS THE YEAR
the Muslims take control of a large area of the Iberian Peninsula, which was integrated into the Umayyad Caliphate under the name of Al-Ándalus.

Temples prior to the cathedral
James the Apostle was buried in a Roman mausoleum next to which, around the year 834, a modest church was built, replaced shortly after, during the reign of Alfonso III, by a three-nave basilica.

The original Roman sepulchre

Church commissioned by Alfonso II

The basilica of Alfonso III

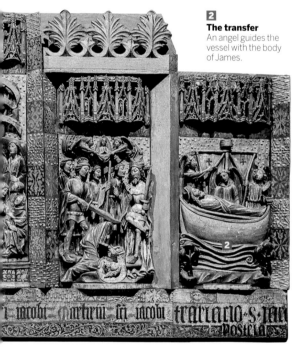

2
The transfer
An angel guides the vessel with the body of James.

Alfonso II the Chaste
He ordered the building of a church to hold Saint James' remains.

820
IS ESTIMATED TO BE THE YEAR
that Bishop Teodomiro found the tomb of James the Apostle.

James the Apostle's tomb
It is situated below the cathedral's high altar.

The original sepulchre

The most widespread story assures that James was buried a few kilometres from the Galician coast, in the mausoleum of a Roman woman named Atia Moheta. On this site his disciples Athanasius and Theodore were also buried, whose tombs flank the apostle's. Hidden by bushes, the mausoleum went unnoticed until the beginning of the 9th century, when it was discovered by Bishop Teodomiro of the diocese of Iria Flavia.

Resistance against the Muslim advance
Established mainly in Gaul, the Franks prevented the Muslims from advancing into Europe after the Battle of Poitiers, in the year 732.

754
IS THE YEAR
Asturias took control of Galicia, which from then on was only subject to sporadic attacks from the Muslims.

The peak of the Asturian Kingdom
Alfonso III consolidated the territorial expansion of Asturias in the latter half of the 9th century. His kingdom was succeeded by that of León.

Viking attacks
Between the 9th and 11th centuries Galicia was subject to diverse raids from Scandinavian warriors, who settled for a time in the territory.

Centre of the city
Jacobean cult is the origin of the city of
Santiago de Compostela, whose urban
layout is organised around the cathedral.

The Way of Saint James

Despite its remote location, the apostle's tomb soon attracted pilgrims from all over Europe, in such a way that different routes were devised which were then equipped with specific guest houses and hospitals.

The rise in pilgrims
The granting of the privilege of the Jubilee or Saint year that was bestowed in 1122 by Pope Callixtus II on the Cathedral of Santiago de Compostela boosted the pilgrimages made by worshippers that wanted to atone for their sins.

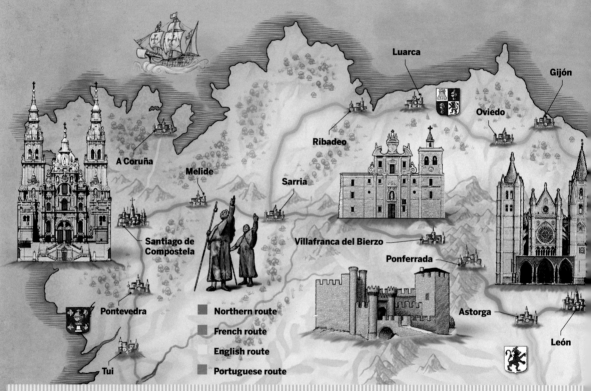

Luarca

Gijón

Oviedo

Ribadeo

A Coruña

Melide

Sarria

Santiago de Compostela

Villafranca del Bierzo

Ponferrada

Pontevedra

Astorga

León

Tui

- Northern route
- French route
- English route
- Portuguese route

HISTORY

The worship of relics

Present in the first Christian communities, the devotion to martyrs gathered force in the Middle Ages by means of the pilgrimage movement.

The martyrium
Based on a central ground plan, this type of building was developed in the Paleo-Christian period in order to worship the memory of a martyr or conserve remains.

Jerusalem
The city converted into the most important objective of Christian pilgrimage by conserving holy places related to Christ such as the Holy Sepulchre.

Exchange routes

The news of the discovery of James the Apostle's tomb spread like wild fire throughout Christian Europe, resulting in a constant growth of pilgrims of diverse origin, who counted on the support of eclesiastical institutions and the monarchy, who instigated the construction of pathways, bridges, accommodation and hospitals to assist travellers. Contributing to the consolidation of Christian kingdoms, numerous development projects sprang up around the main pilgrimage routes, where traders and craftsmen settled and who established networks of economic and cultural exchange which decisively influenced in the religious architecture of the period.

Santillana del Mar

Llanes

Cantabrian part of the route

Santander

San Sebastián

Bordeaux

Bilbao

Irún

Roncesvalles

Saint Jean Pied de Port

Pamplona

Santo Domingo de la Calzada

Logroño

Sangüesa

Puente la Reina

Jaca

Burgos

Belorado

11th century bridge over the River Arga

1099
IS THE YEAR in which the Crusaders conquered the City of Jerusalem, after Pope Urban II had demanded the liberation of the Holy Land.

Rome
Just like Jerusalem, the capital city was to receive the earliest Christian pilgrimages owing to the presence of the tombs of the apostles Saint Peter and Saint Paul.

Canterbury
During the Middle Ages the English town converted into the starting point of the *Vía Francígena*, which spanned 1,700 kilometres until reaching Rome in Italy.

The spread of Jacobean cult

Guarded in the cathedral's archive, texts such as the 'Codex Calixtinus' and the 'Tumbo A' disseminated the worship of James the Apostle, contributing to the consolidation of the pilgrimages.

← **Diffuse authorship**
The Codex Calixtinus was probably the work of cathedral scribes and it included monk Aymeric Picaud's participation, secretary to Pope Calixtus II.

Early testimonies

Written in the 12th century, the *Codex Calixtinus* and *Tumbo A* echoed the tradition that links Saint James to the Iberian Peninsula, reflected in documents prior to the discovery of the sepulchre, such as the texts signed by Saint Isidore of Seville and Saint Beatus of Liébana in the seventh and eighth centuries.

← **'Turpin Chronicle'**
Within the *Codex Calixtinus*, this book tells how James the Apostle appeared before the Emperor Charlemagne.

→ **James in the 'Codex Calixtinus'**

The medieval cathedral

The veneration of the remains of James the Greater led to the design of a large temple in the 11th century, in whose labourious construction participated several sponsors and master builders of diverse origin.

Diego Gelmírez
Papal legate to Spain as well as first Archbishop of Santiago de Compostela, he succeeded Diego Peláez and was the main promoter of the Romanesque cathedral.

The start of the building work

In the year 997, Muslim troops, headed by the *caudillo* Almanzor, destroyed the basilica that Alfonso III had erected to hold the relics of James the Apostle. Although it was rapidly rebuilt, the small temple proved unable to cope with the constant influx of pilgrims, for which reason, in 1075, Bishop Diego Peláez, with the economic support of the King of Léon, Alfonso VI –who was interested in uniting his territory by means of the figure of the apostle–, started upon the construction of a Romanesque style cathedral, designed by the master builder Bernardo el Viejo and his assistant, Galperinus Robertus.

A reference temple
Constructed between the eleventh and twelfth centuries, the Cathedral of Santiago was one of the largest in Medieval Europe.

1105
IS THE YEAR
in which the chapels of the apse were consecrated, where building work started off.

Cross of devotion
The cathedral was finished in 1211, when it was consecrated in the presence of King Alfonso IX.

1112
IS THE YEAR
in which, during the transept's construction, Alfonso III's basilica was demolished.

Towers
With a cubic shape, they were erected at different levels over the cornice of the larger nave.

The north façade
It is the main pilgrim entrance.

GROUND PLAN. LATIN CROSS

The Cathedral of Santiago de Compostela adopted a Latin cross ground plan, formed by two arms of three naves each and an ambulatory that went around the high altar.

Steps
They overcome the uneven land.

The Glory Portico

Romanesque arches of the interior

Close-up of stone choir of Master Mateo

3 Cimborrio
It is over the crossing of the cathedral.

4 Buttresses
Attached to the exterior part of the walls, they allowed the distribution of transverse loads.

Work by phases

After the intervention of master builder Bernardo, work on the cathedral slowed down due to Diego Peláez's dismissal in 1088. With Master Esteban a second phase of work started on the ambulatory and the crossing, while the arrival in 1095 of whom would become the temple's great developer, Diego Gelmírez, gave the final impetus to the cathedral, whose western stretch was built by Master Mateo from 1168.

5 Crenellations
The cathedral was fortified in order to avoid possible sieges.

⊙ Symbolic decoration
The diverse doors of the cathedral have allegorical sculptures.

50 STONEMASONS
initially worked on the building of the cathedral.

17th century's west façade and chevet

Paradise Façade
Apart from being the stage for liturgical acts
and pilgrim rites, the cathedral area attracted
the skills of craftsmen and merchants.

02 | A MILESTONE IN RELIGIOUS ARCHITECTURE
The cathedral of James the Apostle

The city's temple is a reflection of the evolution of society and the economy during the Middle Ages.

During the Middle Ages, the technological innovations in the agricultural world such as the introduction of plough wheels and watermills, amongst other developments, generated a surplus in production that led to an increase in trade and, in consequence, growth in the cities, where architectonic projects of great magnitude began to be erected, such as the great cathedrals. These building milestones, which were furthermore a direct consequence of the growing influence of the ecclesiastical institutions, coincided at the time with a reinterpretation of Christian doctrine and the establishment of the idea that the salvation of the soul was only obtainable by

following the teachings of the Gospel and by attending church, with the repercussion that the new cathedrals became centres of catechetical instruction and worship. This pastoral vocation was reflected in the monumental character of the Cathedral of Santiago de Compostela, which acted as the main element of urban identity not only for its religious activity but for its economic, administrative, educational and festive activity. Due to this interaction with its surroundings, the cathedral transcended its function as headquarters of the diocese and as place of custody for the apostle's remains in order to convert into the most influential construction within the territory.

Obradoiro Façade
The Baroque refurbishment of the temple introduced abundant decoration in order to highlight its symbolic importance.

Silver urn
Located in the crypt that was fitted out in the 19th century below the high altar, it holds James' and his two disciples' remains.

The perfect temple

Santiago de Compostela's cathedral manages to meet the needs generated by the apostolic cult by means of a design of monumental character, a landmark in religious architecture.

Symbolism and functionalism

The final stop on the pilgrimage of the *Way of Saint James* –deemed the most significant religious and cultural movement of the Middle Ages–, the temple is considered a masterpiece of religious architecture (despite its design having a number of constraints arising from the need to accommodate numerous worshippers) for both its interior organisation, which makes the constant stream of pilgrims possible without interrupting liturgical acts, as for the narrowness of its elevation, its harmonious proportions and the integration of numerous decorative elements in an ensemble that is a monumental symbol of the apostle's glory.

✳ **Contrast**
The different façades of the cathedral hide the real structure of this monumental building, where sober forms of medieval origin abound.

Apostolic tomb
The Obradoiro Façade underlines the exaltation of the figure of Saint James by means of allegorical details.

2 **Access stairways to the cathedral**

8,300
SQUARE METRES
is the approximate surface area that the cathedral area takes up.

← **Glory Portico**
Presided by the sculpture of Christ the Redeemer, it implied the culmination of the medieval cathedral.

1 **The Rattle Tower**
It rises 74 metres above Obradoiro Square.

Granite sheet roof

← **Capitals**
Many of the columns have botanical details, a typical decoration from the Romanesque style.

The cathedral's chevet

5

6

4

4
Cimborrio
In the centre of the transept, at its base is the mechanism from which the Botafumeiro (Censer) hangs.

5
Clock tower
Crowned by a lantern, it is located between Quintana Square and Platerías Square.

6
Gallery of the transept

Polychrome angel
It forms part of the decoration of one of the two organs of the of the cathedral, built in the 18th century.

3
NAVES
give shape to the central body of the cathedral, the same number as in the transept.

Transept's central nave

High altar

The interior
Designed to create an intimate atmosphere, the cathedral's interior responds to a symbolic scheme, often used in medieval religious architecture, of a transition space between Earth –represented by the temple's three portals– and Heaven –the high altar that indicates the site of the apostle's remains–.

The cloister's exterior façade

7
Cloister balcony

Verticality
Acting as a symbolic link between Earth and Heaven, the cathedral dedicated to Saint James rises above the city's constructions.

A summation of styles

Designed in the Middle Ages according to the canons of Romanesque architecture, the Cathedral of Santiago de Compostela has undergone numerous renovations conditioned by the trends prevailing in each period.

Intermittent building work

The Cathedral of Santiago de Compostela presupposed the culmination of Romanesque architecture by harmoniously incorporating elements such as the Latin cross plan, the ambulatory and radial chapels. However, the balance of the medieval building was rapidly altered by a series of refurbishments which, especially in the seventeenth and eighteenth centuries, entailed significant changes both outside and inside the temple. Developed intermittently and with no master plan, these renovations made possible the introduction of features belonging to Renaissance, Baroque and neo-Classical styles in a cathedral that, at the same time, became the reflection of the ideological evolution of the institutions involved in its operation.

1 Obradoiro Façade

2 The Rattle Tower

3 Medieval base of the tower

9.5 METRES
is the width of the base of the towers of the Obradoiro.

4 Clock
Located in the tower that it lends its name to, it was designed by Domingo de Andrade.

5 James the knight
This coat of arms on the Treasury Façade depicts the apostle as a warrior.

Bell tower

Watch Tower

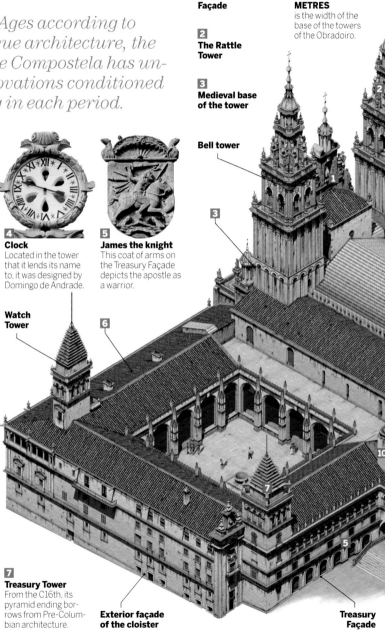

7 Treasury Tower
From the C16th, its pyramid ending borrows from Pre-Columbian architecture.

Exterior façade of the cloister

Treasury Façade

Cloister. Built in the 16th century to substitute the medieval work, it has plateresque details.

8
Chevet
The decorated balustrades and pinnacles hide the Romanesque construction.

9
Chapel of Our Lady of the Pillar
Crowned by a lantern and built in the C18th.

10 Platerías Façade

11 Azabachería Façade

Interior of the Holy Doorway

1649
IS THE YEAR
José Vega y Verdugo arrived in Santiago, instigator of the Baroque remodelling.

12
The cimborrio
Of Gothic origin, its exterior was refurbished by architect José Peña de Toro in the 17th century.

13
The Holy Doorway
The *Puerta Santa* shows figures from the Bible.

The entrances

With the aim of instructing its visitors, the medieval cathedral established a single iconographic discourse with its 3 main doorways: the north one (the Azabachería with the largest number of pilgrims) symbolised the *Fall of Man* and the start of the *Redemptive Promise*; the south one (Platerías) represented the *Fulfilment* of that promise after the *Arrival of the Messiah*, and the west one (Obradoiro) refers to the *Final Judgement* and the *Celestial Jerusalem*. This account was altered by the Baroque remodeling, which demolished and concealed two of the original façades to reinforce the worship of St. James on the new portals.

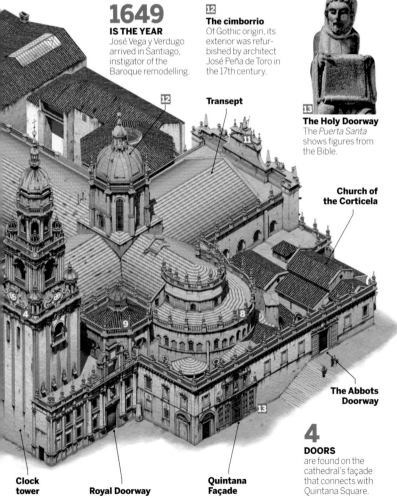

Transept

Church of the Corticela

The Abbots Doorway

12

11

8

4

9

13

4
DOORS
are found on the cathedral's façade that connects with Quintana Square.

Clock tower

Royal Doorway

Quintana Façade

13

The central nave
The austere character of the structure of medieval origin contrasts with the exuberance of the Baroque decorative elements.

Harmonious dimensions

The cathedral's interior hides the original Romanesque style structure, which uses diverse architectonic resources to give shape to a spacious temple.

Cupola

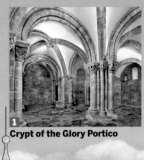

1
Crypt of the Glory Portico

97
METRES
is the cathedral's length, starting from the Glory Portico and ending at the Chapel of Salvador.

22
METRES
is the maximum height that the central nave of the cathedral reaches, while the lateral ones reach 9.5 m.

Clock tower

Medieval base

Cimborrio
It illuminates the crossing.

2
James' tomb
The remains of the apostle are located in a mausoleum situated below the high altar.

Balustrade of the chevet

3
Arches of the tribune

4
Central nave

5
Base of the cimborrio

Tribune
Over the lateral naves there is a gallery that goes around the interior perimeter of the cathedral.

Barrel vault
The central nave roof is reinforced with transverse arches, a Romanesque resource.

Decorative pinnacle

Ribbed vault of the tribune

James the Apostle

6
Bell tower
With a square base of medieval origin, the upper section has a diminishing structure that underlines the verticality of the façade.

7
Glory Portico
Structured around three arches, it constitutes the western closing of the naves.

03 | A HETEROGENEOUS ARRANGEMENT
The cathedral exterior

The monumentality of the façades symbolically reinforces the importance of the cult of James the Apostle.

The exterior of a Christian temple obeys a complex symbolic structure where its architecture is often provided with indoctrinating messages, used as a means of instruction. Façade orientation is one of the key aspects, as light, which represents God, is sought to reinforce the allegorical character of the different sides of the temple. Thus, the apse, the most important area, faces the sunrise, whilst the main façade, faces the sunset, so the route from the main façade to the chevet becomes a spiritual journey from darkness to salvation. The original idea for the cathedral's façades followed this symbolic plan, which was modified by successive alterations to facilitate and reinforce the worship of the apostle. From the original Romanesque project the south portal (the Platerías) remains visible, as well as the layout of the towers on the western façade (the Obradoiro). It is on this second façade where Baroque influence is more evident, the main style used on the temple's exterior following the remodelling plan developed during the 17th and 18th centuries, which affected the finishing of the chevet, the Clocktower and the Azabachería Façade. This summation of disparate constructions gave rise to an eclectic building which found its unity in the reflection of the importance of the cult of Saint James.

Obradoiro Façade
The medieval sculptures that flank the entrance to the crypt contrast with the Baroque decoration.

Capitals of the Platerías doors
One of the few decorative elements conserved from the exterior of the Romanesque cathedral.

The Obradoiro Façade

The most recognisable image of the temple is a granite and glass façade that hides the original Romanesque façade and highlights the monumentality of the arrangement.

Symmetry and verticality

The cathedral's western façade is a Baroque masterpiece which takes its name from the large adjacent square where the temple's stonemasons' workshops were located. Its architect, Fernando de Casas Novoa, embarked on the construction of a new façade in the year 1738 owing to the poor state the Glory Portico was in. The intervention took the form of a pyramidal central body with large windows which joined up with the two existing towers in order to create a symmetrical whole. Moreover, by employing profuse ornamentation, Casas Novoa managed to highlight the upward nature of his work, which was also assisted by the Corinthian columns and the progressive narrowing of the central columns and towers.

91
CARTS came to be used at the same time in order to transfer the granite used on the façade.

1
James the Apostle over the façade

2
The Rattle Tower is on the left-hand side

3
On the right-hand side is the Bell Tower

↻
The original façade
On the upper section of the central body is a large rose window that lights up the inside of the temple.

Cupola decorative end

4
Doors
The double doors are decorated with nails.

5
Athanasius
James' disciple appears dressed as a pilgrim, like the Apostle.

Metal cross

Pinnacle

6
Window
This is one of the largest glass constructions carried out prior to the Industrial Revolution.

3

7
Angels
They carry signs and a cross of James.

7
METRES
is the height which the terrace-belvedere is situated at in the façade's entrance.

Star
It refers to the discovery of James' tomb.

1750
IS THE YEAR
the façade was completed, a few months after the death of Casas Novoa.

10
Hispanic king
He bows at James the Apostle's feet in prayerful actitude.

Reinforcement body of the tower

Privileged space. The different levels of the land meant the Obradoiro Façade could be a few metres higher than the square, thus highlighting its predominant position in the urban surroundings.

8
Romanesque sculpture of King Solomon

9
Entrance stairway

An inclusive work
The construction of the Obradoiro Façade helped unify the elements that had appeared in the early 17th century on the western flank of the temple, such as the reinforcement added to the Belltower and the double-ramped staircase that embellished the entrance to the Glory Portico. Designed by Ginés Martínez, both works were respected by Fernando de Casas Novoa, who also adapted to the previous intervention of the architects José Peña de Toro and Domingo de Andrade with the decorative ending of the belltower. Likewise, the new façade harmoniously fitted in with the attached square, consolidated as a monumental public space.

The exaltation of the Jacobean cult

With the idea of emphasizing the importance of the cathedral in Catholic consciousness, architect Casas Novoa designed the Obradoiro Façade as a great altarpiece decorated with reliefs and sculptures related to Saint James.

The spire
It supports a cross.

1
James
Located in a recess, the apostle appears represented as a pilgrim, carrying a staff and wearing a cape.

Triumphal arch

The rank of James as Patron Saint of the kingdoms of Spain was contested throughout the 17th century, when diverse religious congregations revindicated the importance of other figures such as Saint Michael and Saint Teresa. To counteract this opposition, the Obradoiro Façade was devised as a monumental stone altarpiece dedicated to the reaffirmation of the Jacobean cult, in such a way that all the sculptural decoration planned by architect Fernando de Casas Novoa is related to James and the relics guarded in the cathedral. The apostolic apotheosis is located in the central section of the façade, which acquires the shape of a triumphal arch presided over by the sculptures of Saint James (revered by two kings) and his disciples Athanasius and Theodore that flank the tomb associated to the origin of the cathedral.

＊
Dynamism
The decoration generates a play of light and shadow that adds to the sensation of movement.

7
SCULPTORS
worked on the Obradoiro Façade, including José Gambino and Francisco Lens.

2
Crosses
They refer to the Order of Saint James.

Floral decoration

Knocker on the entrance doors

ARCHITECTURE. THE USE OF GLASS

With the aim of illuminating the interior of the cathedral, Casas Novoa planned large glass windows that generate a mirror effect by reflecting over Obradoiro Square the light they receive during the day, thus highlighting the symbolic character of the façade.

The glass reflects the sky

Sculptures
Saint James' parents and brother are represented on the façade, as well as Saint Susan and Saint Barbara, two martyrs that count on a great following in the city and whose relics are conserved in the cathedral.

Cornices
They are decorated with volutes.

Spherical decorative end

James the Lesser
Sculpted by Gregorio Fernández, the figure that represents the apostle is located in the buttress of the belltower.

3
The kings
James is flanked by two figures that symbolise the devotion that the Spanish monarch professed for the Apostle.

4
Representation of the Apostle's tomb

23
METRES
is the maximum width that the central body of the Obradoiro Façade reaches.

5
Athanasius and Theodore
They guard the tomb.

Ornamental column

Military symbols

Capital with floral decoration

The Obradoiro towers

In the latter half of the seventeenth century the two Romanesque towers on the original western façade were remodelled and acquired greater protagonism thanks to the exuberant Baroque style decoration.

⟲
Decoration
The two towers of the Obradoiro display reliefs with elements associated to James the Apostle, such as the shell, the cross and the star.

Medieval base

The original façade of the cathedral had two square-based towers (the south one higher than the north one), in line with the model of tower popular in the Middle Ages. Their structure underwent few changes until the second half of the 17th century, when – following guidelines set by Canon José Vega y Verdugo– architects José Peña del Toro and Domingo de Andrade renovated the south tower, constructing the balustrade and the section that houses the belltowers and which provides the tower with its name. This intervention was followed by the lengthening of the north or Ratchet Tower, while the refurbishment came to its culmination in the 18th century led by Fernando de Casas Novoa, who designed the stylised decorative ending of both towers, resorting to volutes and pinnacles that combined with the Baroque decoration of the central body of the Obradoiro Façade.

74
METRES
is the height of the two towers, 18 metres more than the central body of the façade.

Weather vane
The crosses that crown the two towers have an arrow that points the direction the wind is blowing.

⟲
The bells
They are on the section that in the 17th century was added to the medieval structure of the south tower.

DESIGN. THE RATCHET

➔
Symbolism
Instrument made up of 4 cross-shaped resonance boxes, the ratchet is a kind of rattle used on Good Friday to recall the Death of Christ.

➔
Functioning
The handle of the ratchet moves a cog, responsible for tensing the reeds that generate the sound of the instrument.

2010
IS THE YEAR
in which an exact replica of the original ratchet was constructed, using chestnut for the sound boards.

The Platerías Façade

Organised around two doors built in the 12th century, the cathedral's southern façade conserves original Romanesque elements as it was the only one that was not concealed during the temple's Baroque refurbishment.

4
Angel
The doors of the façades are flanked by sculptures of angels that sound their trumpets, a possible reference to the Final Judgement.

Gelmírez's project

The Platerías Façade, which is named after the silversmiths that worked in the square, is the only façade of medieval origin that the Cathedral of Santiago de Compostela preserves, though diverse interventions in its ornamentation altered its original appearance. The façade was built between 1103 and 1117 in the framework of the construction program outlined by Archbishop Diego Gelmírez, whose palace was on the southern side of the temple. In this way, the façade acted as a nexus with episcopal power, as well as being the space used for city hall trials. The ensemble is structured around a trumpet-shaped double door with semicircular arches and an upper frieze, which just like the tympanums is profusely decorated, while the two windows with lobed arches preside over the second level of the cathedral's façade.

1
Metopes
Located on the frieze of the façade, they are decorated with star-shaped flowers.

2
Marble columns
Their shafts are decorated with characters from the Bible.

3
The Flagellation of Christ

5
Lobed arches
Their design could be product of the influence of Muslim architecture.

6
Pinnacle
The balustrade that crowns the façade is fruit of the Baroque refurbishment.

Lantern
It guides the pilgrims in the Jacobean years.

7

The Clock Tower
Crowned by a Baroque structure from the 17th century, its medieval base acted as a buttress in order to support the cathedral's south end .

1117
IS THE YEAR
in which the Platerías Façade caught fire during a popular revolt.

8

The scallop
It supports the stair that connects the rooms of the Treasury with the cathedral's south wing.

2.95
METRES
is the approximate width of each one of the doors of the Platerías Façade.

9

Sculpture of the Annunciation
Of Gothic style, the representation of the Virgin is on the last level of the façade.

ARCHITECTURE
The Treasury Façade
The Platerías Façade adjoins the eastern end of the cloister, designed by Rodrigo Gil de Hontañón in the first half of the sixteenth century.

Three sections. The first level of the Treasury Façade presents large semicircular arcades, while on the intermediate level there are windows and on the upper level there is a gallery of archways.

Medallions
Of Renaissance style, the sculptures represent biblical figures and characters linked to the story of Saint James.

10
STEPS
make up the coronation of the Treasury Tower.

Treasury Tower
It could be inspired by the Mausoleum at Halicarnassus or by the Pyramid of Niches.

Point of reference
Built in 1825, the Fountain of the Horses presides over Platerías Square, which leads to some of the busiest streets.

Door decoration

The divine and human nature of Jesus Christ is one of the main themes of the Platerías Façade, which includes sculptures that weren't part of the original design.

The Arrival of the Messiah

The chaotic decoration of the cathedral's Platerías Façade is due to the changes undergone in the year 1117 following a fire and the addition of elements from other parts of the temple, such as the Paradise Façade. That is to say, scenes are interspersed without any apparent thematic unity, above all on the frieze, presided over by Christ and the apostles. However, the two tympanums over the doors have a much more defined iconographic message, which has been related to the fulfillment of the messianic promise that the Paradise Façade announced. The left-hand tympanum shows the temptations of Christ while the right one shows scenes from the Passion, thus forming an ensemble that refers to a human and divine Messiah.

Temptations of Christ
The left tympanum depicts fight between Jesus and the Devil.

⬆
Sculptural disparity
The distribution of the elements on the façade is a reflection of its eventful history.

Devils
Evil is represented on the Platerías Façade with animal figures, such as monkeys and snakes.

Alternation
The outer columns are made from marble, while the inner ones are granite.

⬅
Temptations of Christ
The left tympanum depicts fight between Jesus and the Devil.

4
Modillions
The roof over the frieze is supported by historiated corbels.

11
COLUMNS
frame the entrance doors, three of which are marble.

The angel of the arrest
It swoops down to crown Jesus, arrested by the Romans.

6
Biblical characters decorate the jambs

7
Annunciation scene

Capitals
They combine the floral motifs with depictions of beasts and scenes taken from the Bible.

1115
IS THE YEAR
in which the statues of the frieze are sculpted to be used possibly on the western door.

ICONOGRAPHY
The temptation
The Platerías Façade has diverse sculptures, some of them originating from the Door of the Paradise, which refer to the weakness of the human being.

Cast from Paradise. Adam and Eve are punished for trying the forbidden fruit.

The adulterous woman or Eve
An enigmatic female character holds the skull of her lover in her hands.

Carrier of sin and death

The centaur. Its arrows point at a mermaid, in a composition symbolising the constant struggle between good and bad.

Diverse origin

Amongst the numerous theories existing about the origin of the statues that altered the original iconographic program of the Platerías Façade, the most frequent ones refer to the primitive Paradise Façade (the present Azabachería) and to a project that was probably not carried out on the façade of the western side of the temple (where masterbuilder Mateo constructed the Portico of Glory) dedicated to the *Transfiguration of Jesus Christ*, which the white marble sculpted figures of the apostle James, Moses and Abraham on the frieze must have belonged to.

Clocktower

Starting with a tower of medieval origin, architect Domingo de Andrade erected a structure with a decreasing shape comprised of two sections adorned with floral elements and the Jacobean theme.

← **Bell**
Popularly known as Berenguela, the tower's original bell, which weighs around fourteen tonnes, is on display in the cloister of Santiago de Compostela's cathedral.

Squared and octagonal base

On the intersection of the Platerías and Quintana, the Clocktower was one of the first elements that altered the homogeneity of the cathedral. The development of neighbouring districts on the south side of the temple contributed to the erection of a tower in the fifteenth century that, apart from highlighting the temple's presence in the town, was spacious enough to hold a bell given as a gift by French King Louis XI. From 1676 to 1680 architect Domingo de Andrade carried out the tower's refurbishment, and connected the medieval structure with a highly ornate arcade, with a squared base which in turn connects with an octagonal prism that the dome rests on along with the lantern that is lit during the Holy Years.

Work of Andrade, the clock face is located above the God Chronos

72
METRES
is the height of the Clocktower, whose base spans a width of eleven metres.

Angel
It decorates an arch corbel over which the completion date of the tower is inscribed.

→ **Innovative design**
On the upper section, empty space acquires as much protagonism as the structural and decorative elements.

← **Coat of arms**
The decoration planned by Andrade for the clocktower combines traditional Jacobean motifs with heraldic reliefs.

1831

IS THE YEAR
Archbishop Rafael de Vélez commissions a new mechanism for the clock.

Floral decoration

Relief of the scallop shell

Military trophies

The Quintana Façade

In order to hide the apsidioles that confer an uneven appearance to the medieval cathedral's chevet, in the seventeenth century Canon José Vega y Verdugo instigated the construction of a uniform enclosure.

Plaque in honour of James the Apostle
It is situated below the pedestal that crowns the façade of the Royal Door, designed by Domingo de Andrade in order to support a sculpture of Saint James the Greater decked out as a warrior on horse-back.

Royal Door

A wall as backdrop and vestibule

One of the interventions requested by José Vega y Verdugo was the concealment of the exterior of the cathedral's chevet, which had an irregular design due to the presence of numerous apsidioles and doors. Thus, in 1658, architect José Peña de Toro set about working on enclosing the temple in a uniform way, building the stone walls that make up the façade and the cupola on the cimborrio. After the culmination of the refurbishment led by Domingo de Andrade, the final result was a Baroque arrangement divided into two different canvases –where the Royal Door and the Holy Door stand out– that form a large entrance hall to Santiago Cathedral.

Fruit
The Royal Door as well as the Holy Door have fruit decorations similar to that of the Clocktower with the aim to symbolise 'abundance' so often associated to the patronage of James the Apostle.

1700

IS THE YEAR
architect Domingo
de Andrade fin-
ished the construc-
tion of the Royal
Door, devised as
entranceway for
processions
and grand ceremo-
nies held in
the cathedral.

Jacobean symbols
The façade of the Roy-
al Door is decorated
with medallions with
the cross and tomb.

Military trophies
They refer to the
Apostle's condition as
soldier of Christ.

5

2
Holy Door

3
**Door of the
Archconfraternity
of the Apostle**

4
Door of the Abbots
It connects with
the interior of the
chevet and the Chapel
of the Corticela.

5
**Balustrade with
pinnacles and balls**
It acquired the func-
tion of gallery in the
celebrations that
took place in the
during the Holy Year.

18

STEPS
make up divide Quin-
tana Square into two:
that of the "Dead"
(above) and that of
the "Living" (below).

Stair

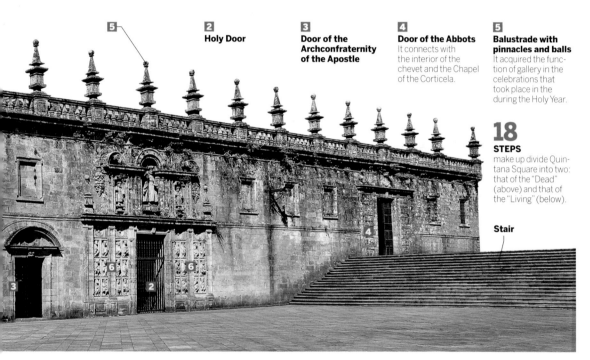

Flowers
Located above some
windows, their petals
adopt the shape of a
windmill.

Blind windows
A clear proof of
the façade curtain
function.

1611

IS THE YEAR
Quintana Square
was developed,
formerly used as a
cemetery.

Sculptures
They are from Master
Mateo's workshop.

The Holy Door

Crowned by the figures of James the Apostle and his disciples Athanasius and Theodore, Quintana Façade's most symbolic entrance is framed by sculptures of biblical characters proceding from the medieval chorus.

Athanasius
James' disciple appears dressed as a pilgrim, like the Apostle and Theodore. The three figures were sculpted by Pedro del Campo in the year 1694.

The Holy Year entrance way

The Holy Door fulfils a liturgical function, given that it is only opened in the Holy Years or during Jubilee, when the Feast of Saint James, celebrated on the 25th of July, falls on a Sunday. The symbolic character of this entrance –which in reality is the backdrop of the original Holy Door, situated in the chevet of the cathedral– is reflected by its structure, which is like the shape of an altarpiece. On the upper part there are three recesses designed by architect Domingo de Andrade which hold the sculptures of James the Apostle and his two disciples, while the ones on either side of the doors are decorated with biblical characters originating from the stone chorus that in the Middle Ages occupied part of the central nave of the cathedral.

Monumentality
Like the Obradoiro Façade, the Holy Door was devised as a triumphal arch that emphasizes the Jacobean cult.

Floral details
Reliefs decorate the sides of the recess of the apostle.

1 Biblical figures
Of medieval origin, they represent apostles, prophets and characters found in the *Old Testament*.

The Azabachería Façade

The present façade on the north side was constructed in the second half of the 18th century in order to replace the former Romanesque façade with a Baroque arrangement that had diverse neo-Classical style elements as well.

Faith
Attributed to sculptor José Gambino, the figure that refers to the first theological virtue presides over the façade's second level, with a chalice and cross of stylised design by Nicolás Vidal.

Three levels

Initially known as the Door of Paradise, the north façade was always the busiest, as it marked the end of the French pilgrimage route. However, in 1758 the canonry decided to demolish the Romanesque façade and commissioned architect Lucas Ferro Caaveiro with the new one, who started the work in Baroque style and who was soon substituted by Domingo Lois Monteagudo, chosen by the Academy of Fine Arts with the aim to introduce neo-Classical resources in the design. Divided into 3 floors, the resultant façade –known as the Azabachería, for the presence of craftsmen in the square that worked with jet or lignite (a mineraloid called *azabache* in Spanish)– was particularly striking for its Greco-Roman character, underlined by the Doric columns on the lower floor and the presence of rosettes and decorative medallions.

St. James
Work of Máximo Salazar, the sculpture of the apostle that crowns the façade has two medieval monarchs at his feet.

Alfonso III of Asturias
He kneels as a sign of submission.

Pilgrim's attire

Ordoño II of León

1769
IS THE YEAR
Lois Monteagudo finished the construction of the façade.

The door
It is decorated with nails and rectangular mouldings.

Archbishop Rajoy coat of arms

Medallion with Christ's face

Canonry coat of arms

Medallion of the Virgin

The roofs. The use of granite plaques converted the roof of the cathedral into a large staircase that could be quite safely walked around by the pilgrims, who in the Middle Ages carried out diverse rites in this space, such as the burning of the attire used during their journey. In the 17th century the roofs were re-clad with tiles, and it wasn't until the 1960's that the original granite was rediscovered. After some renovation work, the roof terrace –which has views of elements of Romanesque construction– reopened to the public in 2004 as part of the museum.

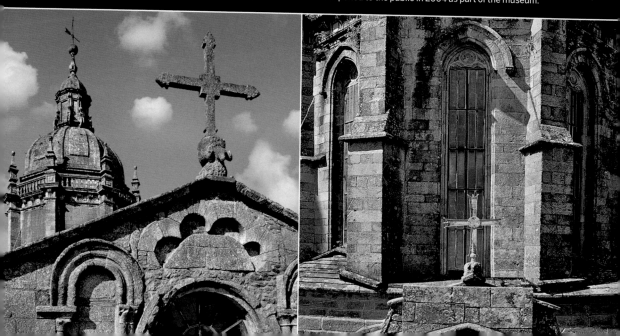

THE WORK OF MASTER BUILDER MATEO

The Glory Portico

A high point of medieval art, the monumental western entrance of the temple represents the triumph of Christ.

During the Middle Ages, the Church converted the pictorial and sculptural representation of concepts and passages taken from the Bible into a very effective way of instructing a mostly illiterate population. This method of indoctrination meant artists had to follow strict guidelines which led to a homogeneous style –disseminated by means of the pilgrimage routes, where influences, work methods and manpower could be interchanged–, in such a way that the façades and walls of European Christian temples eventually took on similar symbolic decoration, based on recurring themes such as the cycle of the *Nativity* and the *Apocalypse of Saint John*. These iconographic programs also shaped the exterior ornamentation of Santiago Cathedral, whose Glory Portico –the architectonic and sculptural ensemble which in the twelfth century culminated the western façade of the temple– resorted to the *Final Judgement* as source of inspiration. A turning point in Medieval European art, the portico is work of Master Mateo, considered the most important artist of the Romanesque period, whose work fortified ideas in other Romanesque churches on the *Way of Saint James* (such as that of Saint-Pierre de Moissac, in France) and, at the same time enhanced the symbolism of the Galician cathedral.

Symbolism
The different sculptural groups on the cathedral's Glory Portico are interrelated and weave a complex religious discourse.

The blasphemer's punishment
A demon pulls out the tongue of a sinner on one of the capitals of the façade behind the Obradoiro Façade.

The culmination of the cathedral

Construction on the Glory Portico began in the twelfth century following the innovative architectonic solution devised by master builder Mateo to counteract the uneven land on the western side of the temple.

Complex work

On the 23rd of February, 1168, King Ferdinand II of León made it known that Master Mateo –of unknown origin– would receive a lifelong pension in order to complete the western side of the Cathedral of Santiago de Compostela. The privilege earned by the architect corresponded with the complexity of the project, since the sloping terrain meant he would have to devise a solution that was based around three distinct levels. In order to get over the unevenness, a crypt was planned, a structure that was unprecedented in Galician architecture at the time and which the Glory Portico is built upon, consisting of three flared arches (one for each of the cathedral's naves) decorated with allegorical sculptures. Lastly, on the upper level, the gallery extension was completed and a vault was added which meant the plans for the crypt and façade could finally come to fruition.

1
The Obradoiro Façade
The Baroque work superimposes the medieval structure.

2
The gallery
It is above the lateral naves.

3
Animals
The bases of the columns are decorated with sculptures of beasts.

4
Narthex
It provided pilgrims with shelter.

5

5
Prophet Daniel
All the figures that decorated the Glory Portico were polychromed.

Terrace-belvedere

Entrance staircase

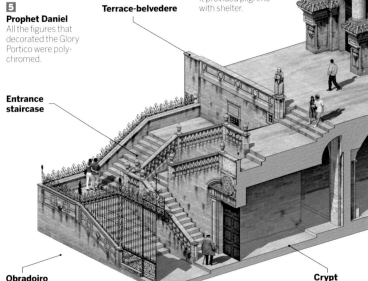

Obradoiro Square

Crypt entrance

➜
Oculus
Flanked by two tetralobulars, it contributes to the illumination of the temple.

Keystone of the gallery vault
The figure of the lamb is the representation of Christ the Saviour.

17
METRES
is the width of the Glory Portico, which reaches a height of 9.5 metres.

Lintels on the Glory Portico
Installed in 1188, when building work was already in full swing, their inscriptions confirm the presence of master builder Mateo.

7
Jesus dominates central tympanum

20
YEARS
is roughly how long it took to construct the Glory Portico of Santiago Cathedral.

8
Crypt
Also known as the 'Old Cathedral' it supports the structure of the Glory Portico.

The pillars distribute the loads

A hybrid style
Master builder Mateo and him team of workers introduced a new style, without precedent in the Iberian Peninsula, which anticipated the characteristics of Gothic art. Although in Mateo's work pure Romanesque elements can still be found, with their characteristic rigidity, in many figures on the Glory Portico –originally polychromed– the new artistic trend can be noted which influences the expressivity of the sculptures and their independence with regard to the architectonic framework that they are in.

Pillar with floral and animal details

Crypt of the Glory Portico

Keystone of crypt vault

The entrance's three archways

Devised as the culmination of the program developed on three other façades of the cathedral, the Glory Portico symbolises the establishment of the Kingdom of God.

The ancients of
the Apocalypse

01

02

Floral decoration

1 Left arch
Both the sculptures of the jambs and the decoration of the archivolts refer to scenes and characters proceding from the *Old Testament*.

2 Central arch
Double the width of the lateral arches and divided by a mullion, it has a tympanum presided over by the figure of a seated Christ.

3 Right-hand arch
Related to the *Final Judgement*, it is distinguished by the longitudinal orientation of the archivolt reliefs, a typically Gothic feature.

16
SCULPTURES
decorate the jambs of the arches. Those on the left of the mullion depict various prophets and to the right, apostles.

03

The central arch

The Glory Portico's main entrance is the only one that has a tympanum, adorned with diverse sculptural groups that refer to passages from the Book of Revelation.

Celestial Jerusalem

With the same width as the main nave, the central arch of the Glory Portico is the only one of the three with a tympanum on its structure. Its monumental size, held up by the mullion that divides the flow of pilgrims entering the temple, is the backdrop for the narration of the *Vision of the Celestial Jerusalem* described in the *Book of Revelation*. Framed by tetramorphs, the representation of the biblical text of Saint John is presided over by the figure of Christ, whose wounds from the *Crucifixion* are on view, an episode which is referred to by the angels located under the sculptures symbolising the souls of the Blessed.

➔ Symbolic dimensions
The sculptures on the tympanum vary in size according to their hierarchy.

3
METRES
is the approximate height of Christ's figure presiding over the central tympanum.

Chosen people
Of varying size, the figures gaze down at Christ in a gesture of prayer.

38
SCULPTURES
represent the Blessed, who are divided into two symmetrical groups.

◀ Expressivity
The expressions on the faces of the angels on the imposts of the central arch are realistically depicted.

Angel with censer

➔
Privileged position
Below the feet of Christ is the figure of James, which crowns the mullion, thus showing the divine favour that he was granted.

1
The Evangelists
They write above the animals that symbolise them, with the exception of Matthew, who is over an abacus.

The musicians

7
METRES
is the approximate measurement of the tympanum base of the central arch.

2
Angels
Those that hold instruments on the Passion Façade that touched Christ's body cover their hands with a veil.

The source of inspiration
The *Book of Revelation* was one of the most recurrent themes of medieval art, given that its promise of reward in the form of eternal life allowed to play down the rules of the prevailing feudal system and, at the same time, to reinforce the hierarchical structure of society, divided into a highly structured class system.

The salvation
An angel crowns the figures that symbolise the souls of God's *Chosen Ones*.

▓▓
ICONOGRAPHY. THE FIGURE OF CHRIST

When carrying out the Glory Portico master builder Mateo moved away from the traditional representation of Christ as an all powerful judge in order to show him instead as a very human figure, showing the marks on his feet and hands to demonstrate the suffering he had undergone.

Pantocrator of Tahull

The elder musicians

Sculpted in great detail, the figures located on the archivolt that is part of the tympanum of the Glory Portico are a representation of the twenty-four elders described by Saint John in the fourth chapter of the Book of Revelation.

Symbolism
In the Middle Ages the Elders of the Apocalypse were related to the union of the *Old* and *New Testament*, when considering that they constituted the representation of the 12 biblical prophets and Jesus' 12 apostles.

Interaction
Dressed in robes and wearing crowns, the elder musicians of the Glory Portico avoid the frontality typical of Roman sculpture and turn their faces so they are facing eachother creating a dynamic arrangement.

Old and young
Although the majority of the musicians have a beard as a sign of their old age, some of the figures are beardless. This representation, remote from the description of the *Apocalypse*, was common in the iconography of the time.

The mullion

Presided over by the figure of James the Apostle, the column dividing the central arch of the Glory Portico into two represents Jesus Christ's genealogical tree.

From Heaven to Earth

The mullion of the Glory Portico is comprised of a collection of columns carved from a single block of granite, to which a marble pillar is attached, skilfully decorated by the workshop of master builder Mateo. By means of diverse groups of figures, the mullion established a symbolic link between the celestial and terrestrial world: the upper part of the arrangement is comprised of a capital dedicated to the temptations of Jesus and is located behind St. James' head, who appears in the second section in contemplative mood; below his feet, a capital with a depiction of the Holy Trinity finishes off a shaft that depicts Christ's family tree; while the base makes up the final section, symbolising the terrestrial by means of Man and beasts.

✻ The Apostle's message
James carries a sign with the words "God sends me", which refers to the idea of redemption.

Master Mateo
With humble gesture, the sculpture behind the mullion might depict the portico's creator.

2
METRES
is the approximate height of the shaft of the mullion, which is made from marble.

↩ The lions
Two creatures in docile stance support the faldstool on which Saint James sits, thus reinforcing the apostle's authority.

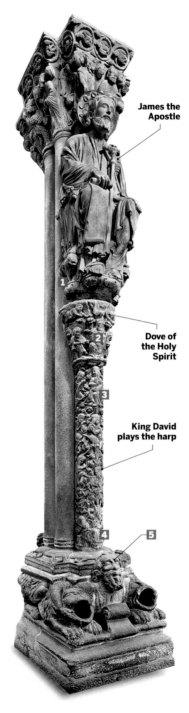

James the Apostle

Dove of the Holy Spirit

King David plays the harp

2 Capital
Angels with censers flank the Holy Spirit and the Father, who holds the Son.

3
DEMONS
appear tempting Christ on the capital situated behind James' head.

Virgin Mary
Wearing a crown similar to that of Jesus of the tympanum, she protects her belly.

Jesse
Recalling Isaiah's prophecy, a tree grows from his chest and goes up the mullion.

5 The man that controlled beasts
The bearded figure has been associated to Adam and Samson.

Master builder Mateo

His origin and training unknown, the
author of the Glory Portico had the best
craftsmen at his disposal in order to
carry out an architectonic project that
would be passed on to posterity.

1
Manufacture of
the sculptures
Made from granite
and polychromed
with drying mineral
oil and proteins.

2
Installment of
the figures
Once created the
sculptures were put
into their definitive
position.

3
Representatives
from the clergy
They supervised
the theological
message.

4
Masterbuilder
Mateo
He presented
the model
and the plan.

55
SCULPTURES
were done by Mateo's workshop in order to decorate the portico's central tympanum.

Capitals.
They were sculpted, and later on, put into position on the portico.

10%
IS WHAT REMAINS
of the original poly-chrome that is on the sculptures of the Glory Portico.

Portico pillars

5
Material
Thick and fine grained granite was used.

The left lateral arch

The Old Testament is the source of inspiration for the archivolts on the doorway, whose reliefs depict the tribes of Israel and the patriarchs that await the Messiah.

Bases
Symbols of the terrestrial world, the beasts located on the base of the columns that support the prophets seem to be crushed by the weight of the ensemble.

Biblical references

The left archway of the Glory Portico, a doorway measuring almost eight metres high on the north lateral nave, is formed by three semi-circular archivolts whose reliefs hark back to the times of the *Old Testament*. Below the florally decorated upper archivolt, the central bend has a set of ten figures carrying scrolls who are trapped by a molding, in a composition that has been interpreted as the subjection of the Jews to the *Law of Moses*; while on the lower semi-circle eleven biblical figures combine with the foliage. In the centre of this level a representation of God stands out that could refer to the *Resurrection*, the moment in which Christ descends to limbo in order that the souls of the righteous can rise to Heaven. In this way, the archway could be interpreted as a prelude of the salvation expressed on the central tympanum.

A molding immobilises the characters on the central curve

Prophets
The sculptures of the jambs probably represented minor prophets such as Abdías and Amos.

Oculus
Over the arch is a round window with the aim to facilitate the illumination of the interior of the temple.

1
Capitals
They vary the floral decoration with compositions comprised of real or mythological creatures.

Lions, symbols of instinct

Capital with floral motifs

A pair of mythological animals

Bird siren, common theme

The right lateral arch

A keystone decorated with Christ's head is the nucleus of the representation of the Final Judgement, in which the Just attain salvation alongside the angels whilst the Sinners are tormented by demons.

Angel
Situated on the left half of the arch, it carries two naked children in its arms, who symbolise the souls free of sin that willl be able to reach divine salvation.

The blessed and the condemned

Following the structure of three archivolts used on the left-hand side lateral door, the right hand-side archway of the Glory Portico refers to the *Final Judgement*, the moment in which –as Saint Matthew in his gospel describes– God decides the fate of the Just and the Sinners. On the archway this scene is presided over by the busts of Jesus Christ and an angel –or possibly Saint Michael, according to various sources– that appear on the keystones of the central and lower archivolt, while on the left hand side of the door are the souls of the Blessed, depicted as children that are carefully watched over by angels; and on the right are the condemned, who are punished by demons. On the upper archivolt there is a set of ten figures who symbolise the souls of the virtuous and the sinful that await the *Final Judgement* in limbo.

Realism
The sculptures of the soul saving angels are provided with quite detailed volumes, such as the folds in their tunics.

13

HUMAN FIGURES
appear on the arch suffering the torments from the demons.

The men and the asses
The figures of this capital symbolise the need to curb one's desires.

ICONOGRAPHY. THE TORMENTS

The scenes of the condemned and the demons on the right half of the arch refer to sins such as gluttony, pride, wrath and avarice by means of compositions that are characterised by their severity.

The demons
They appear like monsters with animal features, in harmony with the representation of evil developed since the ninth century.

Didactic art. On the right lateral arch, the contrast of the angels that symbolise salvation and the demons that punish sinners show the desire of master builder Mateo to provide the Glory Portico with a moralising message, which would arouse deep reflection in those who contemplated the work, in order that they were conscious of the advantages of leading a virtuous life that was accord with the precepts of the church.

The crypt

With a structure similar to that of a basilica, the subterranean space of the western façade completes the message of the Glory Portico, by representing the terrestrial world that is at God's feet.

Beasts
Figures abound in the crypt that are linked to the terrestrial world, a feature that reinforces the theory that this space completes the discourse of the Glory Portico.

Symbolic ornamentation

Accessible from the bottom of the Obradoiro steps and connected with the inside of Santiago Cathedral, the crypt had its origin in the necessity to devise a structure that would get over the drop in land and, at the same time, was able to withstand the weight of the Glory Portico. To carry this task out, master builder Mateo devised a space presided over by a large pillar from which cross vault arches arose and on whose far eastern end is an ambulatory, which has a rectangular ground plan flanked by two absidioles and two niches. With regards to ornamentation, two central vault keystones, decorated with the sun and moon, symbolise the terrestrial world's need for light when awaiting the arrival of the Kingdom of God.

Functionality
It is said that the crypt –which is at present integrated into the Cathedral Museum– was used to carry out liturgical rites.

27.8
METRES
is the total length of the crypt, which reaches a maximum height of 7 metres.

Figure of a capital
Some of the sculptures that decorate the Glory Portico are characterised by their coarse style.

Vault keystone
The plant-life seems to be holding down a man, symbolising the struggle between good and bad.

1
Sun
Clutched by an angel, it is sculpted with large burning flames.

2
Moon
It appears in its first quarter, a symbol of light and growth.

16.8
METRES
is the length of the crossing of the crypt, where the two entrance steps lead to.

3
Witches
A capital is decorated with figures of these mythological beasts with female face and bird-like body.

Capital
In a composition dominated by visual tension, some beasts are trapped by entwining plants.

Differences in style

The sculptural decoration of the crypt has led to diverse theories about the creator of this space, given that only the vault keystones and some of the capitals on the columns present a direct relationship with the style predominant on the Glory Portico. The differences could be due to the fact that the construction of the crypt was carried out at different stages or, on the other hand, was product of the participation of different workshops that worked simultaneously on the project under the direct supervision of Master Mateo.

ARCHITECTURE. ACCESS FROM THE SQUARE

In the 17th century, with the construction of the staircase of the Obradoiro, a reorganisation of the access to the crypt came about, which projected outwards in front of the western façade, whilst in 1738 the entrance took on its definitive design under the refurbishment of Casas Novoa.

The entrance to the crypt

05 | FUNCIONALITY AND SYMBOLISM
Inside the cathedral

The Cathedral of Santiago de Compostela is regarded as a reference model of pilgrimage churches.

By prioritising the shared experience of worship, the early Christians had to develop a building that would fulfill their liturgical requirements, and the solution was to be found in Greco-Roman civil architecture, concretely the basilica, an area of rectangular ground plan divided into three or five naves. Christian basilicas evolved including elements that reinforced the symbolic character of architecture, such as the transept, a nave with the same height as the central one that, by cutting crosswise through the temple, provided a Latin cross style ground plan. The Cathedral of Santiago de Compostela was planned based on this model, which was common in Bene-

dictine monastery churches of the Middle Ages, but it was also endowed with new features such as a spacious interior, vaulted ceilings, cruciform pillars, a cimborio, the profusion of chapels, the presence of an ambulatory and a gallery. Respected in posterior refurbishments of the cathedral, all these elements –also present in other churches built along the Jacobean route – contributed to making Santiago de Compostela a reference model of pilgrimage architecture, which was to reach its peak during the Romanesque period providing the temples of Christian Europe with a homogenous style that united functionality with symbolism.

Worshipper praying

James the knight

⊙
Monumentality
The great height of the central nave, covered by a 22 metre high barrel-vault, creates a sensation of tremendous verticality.

⊙
Clavijo tympanum
Found on the transept, it recreates the Clavijo Battle from the 9th century in which James assisted the Christian troops.

A space for retreat

Considered one of the great medieval works from a dimensional point of view, the cathedral dedicated to Saint James manages to generate, despite its large size, an atmosphere that is conducive to prayer and reflection.

Virgin with Child
The tympanum that presides over the Church of the Corticela's entrance is adorned with the Adoration of the Magi.

Two wide arms
Planned as the largest Romanesque temple on the Iberian Peninsula, the Cathedral of Santiago is organised around a Latin cross ground plan scheme with two crossing arms. The first one, 97 metres long, goes from west to east and directs the worshippers' gaze to the chevet –with reference to the path from the earthly to the divine–; while the other goes from north to south. On the two-armed intersection –each one of them divided into three naves– is the high altar, surrounded by an ambulatory. With this structure, the cathedral could deal with numerous pilgrims and, at the same time, create a space appropriate for worship.

✱ The structure
The temple's interior stands out for its narrowness, emphasised by the triforium over the lateral naves.

Gallery
It goes around the temple.

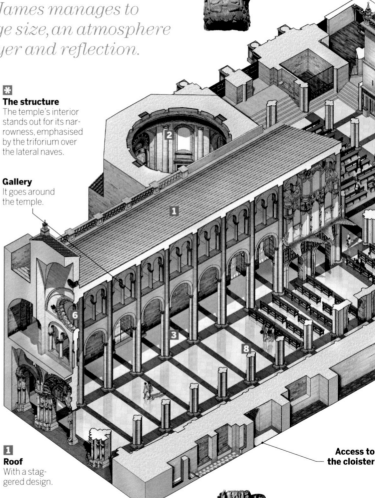

Access to the cloister

2 Chapel of Communion

1 Roof
With a staggered design.

17 CHAPELS
lent to worship are in the cathedral, many of them added in later refurbishments.

3 Pillars
The separation between naves is marked by composite pillars, with columns joined to their shafts.

Floral detail
The organs located on the central nave stand out for their Baroque inspiration.

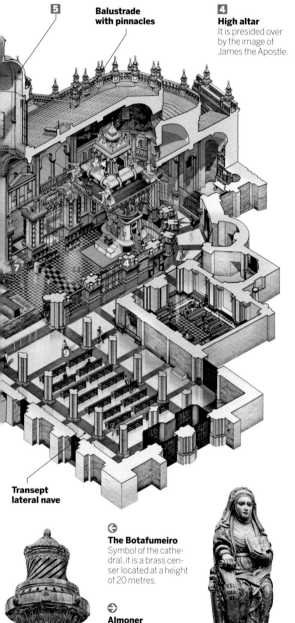

5
Balustrade with pinnacles

4
High altar
It is presided over by the image of James the Apostle.

7

9

4

Transept lateral nave

5
Located on the crossing, the cimborio channels exterior light

6
Tribune of the Glory Portico
The large oculus and the arches take away a lot of the weight from the wall that supports the three arch structure of the lower level.

Illumination

The medieval cathedral had more than a hundred windows distributed around its entire perimeter, with the aim to distribute natural light in a uniform manner within the interior of the temple and provide clarity to the naves as well as the gallery. However, the subsequent renovations notably cut back on illumination with the construction of new elements that blocked off many of the windows.

↶ **The Botafumeiro**
Symbol of the cathedral, it is a brass censer located at a height of 20 metres.

↷ **Almoner**
It depicts Mary Salome, the mother of James the Apostle.

7

8
Central or main nave

9
Transept of the Platerías side

The naves of the main arm

Structured around Romanesque style columns and arches, the three naves that connect the Obradoiro Façade with the chevet of the cathedral act as a majestic covered gallery.

Capital
As a consequence of the shared authorship of the cathedral, the decoration of the columns of the central nave do not adhere to a unique iconographic programme.

Architectonic balance

Despite the construction of the naves being a slow and laboured process that counted on the participation of diverse master builders, the main arm of Saint James Cathedral is characterised for its harmonious design, based on the application of the main principles of Romanesque architecture. Channeler of the visitors coming from Obradoiro, the central nave is separated from the lateral ones by slender pillars of squared base with attached columns that make up the transverse arches of the barrel vault. Covered with groin vaults, the lateral naves are crowned by a triforium, which –apart from accommodating pilgrims and acting as a privileged gallery in grand ceremonies– helps distribute the loads coming from the barrel vault.

The central nave
The perspective created by the composite columns and the barrel vault leads the eye towards the cathedral's altar.

Entrance way to the crypt
It is decorated with a cross that commemorates the devotion of the cathedral.

8.5
METRES
is the average width of the central nave of the cathedral, while the width of the lateral naves is 4.5 metres.

North lateral nave
Connected to the crypt, the stretch near to the Portico of the Glory was built under the supervision of master builder Mateo.

Tied figures

Some authors claim that the nave capitals are work of the master sculptor that carved the figures on the disappeared Paradise Façade, situated on the north side of the cathedral, which is now the present-day Azabachería.

The triforium's arches are rounded

12
METRES

is roughly the height at which the gallery goes around the cathedral's second level.

The gallery receives light from the exterior

Stonemason marks

The workers that participated in the construction of the cathedral left their mark on numerous columns.

1.8
METRES

is the rough measurement of the base of the pillars that separate the naves.

The size of the gallery strengthens its use

ART. MASTER MATEO'S CHOIRSTAND

The central nave was initially taken up by a stone choir gallery, created by the workshop of master builder Mateo, which referred to the *Apocalypse*. New liturgical trends led to its destruction in 1604 and some of its sculptures, were moved to other destinations, such as the Holy Door.

Reconstruction of the choir

The organs of the cathedral

On the last sections of the central nave are two organs constructed in the early 18th century that underline the verticality of the cathedral by means of their pyramidal design.

James
Crowning one of the organs of the cathedral, James the Apostle is on horseback successfully fighting off Muslim soldiers.

Angels
Carved by craftsmen Miguel de Romay and Antonio Alfonsín, the detailed figures that decorate the organ boxes reinforce the iconographic program of the high altar, where the angels take on great protagonism.

Coat of arms of Archbishop Rajoy
It refers to the Prelate that commissioned the construction of the organs, whose decoration was carried out by Miguel de Romay and Antonio Alfonsín following the guidelines set by Domingo de Andrade.

The transept

Of large dimensions, the transversal naves of the cathedral connect the Azabacheria Façade with that of the Platerías, converting into an important centre of circulation of symbolic character.

Atlas
He supports the balustrade going around the cimborio's interior.

Capitals
With a didactic purpose, they recreate scenes of punishments and martyrs.

Differentiating element

The transept is the transversal nave that crosses the main nave in a perpendicular way, providing Romanesque temples with their characteristic Latin cross ground plan. Its name originates from the Latin *septum* (barrier) and symbolically expresses the division between earth, represented by the naves, and heaven, symbolised by the chevet. In Santiago, however, it acquires a new function thanks to its monumental dimensions (65 metres by 20 metres wide). By connecting with the façades of Azabachería and Platerías, the transept acted as a covered passage that allowed the union of the two main hubbubs of activity of the cathedral area and, likewise, became a path of purification for the pilgrims entering the cathedral.

Amplitude
With an approximate width of eight metres, the central nave of the transept can accommodate a large number of worshippers during Mass.

Holy water font
Located on the interior façade of Platerías, it is said that the *Horse of Almanzor* drank from it during the attack in the year 997.

1105
IS THE YEAR
construction on the walls of the transept was finished, carried out by the workshop of craftsmen led by *Maestro* Esteban.

Clavijo tympanum
Located over a blinded window decorated with Jacobean symbols it is considered to be the first representation of James the knight.

James the Lesser
Attached to one of the columns of the crossing, this fifteenth century figure is used to collect donations.

The cimborio

On the intersection of the central nave and the transept there is a cimborio, an element that contributes in large measure to the illumination of the cathedral's interior and, at the same time, underlines the central axis of the religious space. The cupola –which during the Middle Ages was a fortified structure designed to ward off attacks– adopts an octagonal shape connected to the squared base of the crossing by means of bevelled vaults. Their eight ribs come together in a central keystone that is decorated with a rosette, which is hidden by a wooden disc that has pictures which include a symbol of the eye of God.

1
Entrance door to the sacristy
Of Renaissance style, James and Saint Ildefons appear on it.

2
Crossing
The intersection of the transept and the central nave is characterised by verticality.

32
METRES
is how high the cimborio reaches, the maximum height within the temple interior.

Trumpeting angels. Situated on the transverse arches that support the cimborio, the figures are a mix of Romanesque and Gothic style.

The Botafumeiro

Converted into one of the most popular symbols of the cathedral, the great silverplated brass censer that hangs from the cimborio is used to purify the atmosphere during the Eucharist rite.

1.80 m

21.8 m

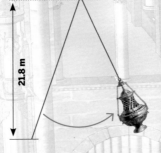

1
The *tiraboleiros* pull the great censer
They energetically swing the censer led by the senior *tiraboleiro*.

2
Oscilation on the crossing
The censer hangs at fifty centimetres from the vault.

3
The speed of the Botafumeiro
The censer reaches 68 kilometres per hour at ground level.

Iron frame

Wooden drums

✳
The support
The mechanism from which the Botafumeiro hangs was created in the 16th century by Juan Bautista Celma.

53
KILOS
is how heavy the cathedral's Botafumeiro weighs, whose height is approximately 94 cms.

1851
IS THE YEAR
in which the present Botafumeiro was built, which was then restored in 2006.

1

The first botafumeiros
From the 13th to 17th century, the censers used were made from silver.

The robbery of the original censer
In 1809 it was pillaged by French troops and was subsituted with an iron one.

The present silver-plated great censer
The botafumeiro used at present was designed in 1851 by silversmith Losada.

2

4

3

4
Iron chains

Incense and coal

Church of the Corticela

Initially a construction independent from the cathedral, the oratory dedicated to Mary has features that give away its pre-Romanesque origin and at the same time includes the touch of master builder Mateo.

Our Lady of Consolation
Of Renaissance style, the sculpture that presides over the main chapel depicts the Virgin Mary wearing a large crown, with Jesus in her arms.

Quadrangular ground plan

Built in the 9th century during the reign of Alfons III and refurbished during the 13th century, the Church of the Corticela was originally an oratory used by the Benedictine monk community from the Monastery of Pinario. Dedicated to the Virgin Mary, the church –planned as a building independent from the cathedral, to whose transept it was later connected by a corridor– conserves characteristics of its pre-Romanesque foundation such as the quadrangular layout, while its façade, decorated with a tympanum that shows a scene from the *Adoration of the Magi*, fits in with the style of master builder Mateo. 12 metres wide by 8.6 metres long, the interior of the church is divided into three naves –the central one, higher than the lateral ones– separated by semicircular arches that rest on columns with Romanesque botanical capitals.

The decoration of an impost

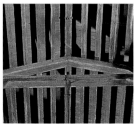

Wooden roof

Tomb of the pilgrim

Cross potent

The nave chapels

The cathedral's successive refurbishments altered the original Romanesque ground plan to fit out numerous chapels of varied typology intended for saint worship and for the tombs of clerics and temple sponsors.

James the Equestrian
A sculpture by José Gambino that depicts the Apostle as a warrior on a horse presides over the Chapel of James the Knight, on the north nave.

Variety of styles
Decorated with striking altarpieces, the chapels that overlook the naves have their origin in different periods of construction. On the north flank of the main arm are the Saint Christ of Burgos and the Communion chapels. The first one, based on a Greek cross ground plan, was built between 1662 and 1664, while the second one dates back to 1719 and adopts a neo-Classical rounded shape. On the cathedral's transept the chapels are concentrated on the Azabachería side. Adorned with altarpieces from the 18th century, the Saint Anthony and Saint Catalina ones flank the door, while around the Church of the Corticela are the chapels dedicated to Saint Andrew –planned in 1674– and the Holy Spirit–of medieval origin and renovated during the Baroque period–. Lastly, the Chapel of Prime, of Renaissance origin, connects with the ambulatory.

**18
METRES**
is the approximate diameter of the Communion Chapel.

Chapel of Prime
A relief from the C18th shows a Christ lowered from the cross.

Chapel of Saint Christ of Burgos

The Communion Chapel
Of neo-Classical style, its cupola is supported by Ionic columns.

Saint Catalina's Chapel

The Holy Spirit Chapel

Saint Anthony's Chapel

Saint Andrew's Chapel

06 | THE MOST SACRED PLACE
The cathedral chevet

Centre of Christian liturgy, the most important section of the temple accentuates the cult of James the Apostle.

Greatly influenced by the round constructions that were added to the main body of Roman buildings, the chevet is in fact the most striking place in a Christian temple as it is where the altar is situated and where the priest carries out the Eucharist rite. Its symbolic importance means that its location is carefully considered, in such a way that it not only has to be visible to the majority of worshippers gathering in the naves, but also face sunrise in order that an association with light can be established, a metaphor for the *Arrival of Christ* and new life. In the Cathedral of Santiago de Compostela, the presence of the tomb that held James the Apostle's

relics delves deeper into the holy character of the chevet, which in the Middle Ages was typically the first part of the temple to was built. Successive refurbishments altered the original Romanesque design with the substitution of some of the medieval chapels and the incorporation of new decorative elements, but they also helped reinforce the importance of this part of the cathedral. In the same vein, the construction of a new Baroque style high altar was undertaken, which culminated the restructuring of the chevet in order to enforce or underline the centrality of the figure of James the Apostle within the cathedral arrangement.

High altar
Of dynamic lines, the ensemble formed by the baldachin and the niche set the stage for the tomb of James the Apostle.

Angel
The polychromed sculptures that hold up the baldachin manage to underline the celestial character of the high altar.

Golden terminations

The temple nucleus

Refurbished to forment the cult of Saint James, the cathedral chevet's layout is based on the crypt that contains the apostle's relics, with the high altar as central nucleus around which seven radial chapels are situated.

Heterogeneous design

Just like on the temple exterior, the Cathedral of Santiago de Compostela's chevet is the result of a number of interventions carried out by diverse master builders and developers that wanted to modernise the most important space in the temple with the aim of strengthening the Jacobean cult. The physical and symbolic centre is the high altar, which by means of its spectacular Baroque design indicates the location of the crypt with the relics of the Apostle James. Surrounding it – and accessible from a generous ambulatory, an architectonic resource typical of the churches of pilgrimage– are seven apsidial chapels that combine original Romanesque features with Gothic, Renaissance, and above all Baroque elements.

✳
Structure
The presence of the crypt means that the altar rises over the level of the ambulatory and the chapels.

1
Altarpiece of the Chapel of Salvador

36
COLUMNS
of Solomonic style decorated with vine shoots mark out the high altar's perimeter.

Saint John's chapel

Chapel of Our Lady the White one

Saint Faith Chapel

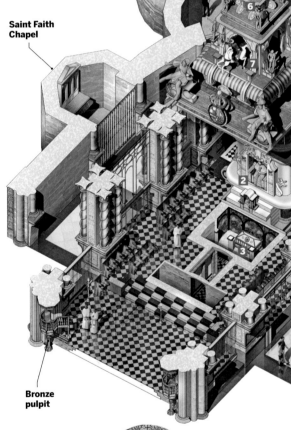

2
High altar

3
James' tomb

Bronze pulpit

3.33
METRES
is the width of the crypt in which the relics of James are laid to rest.

4

↻
Consecration cross
It is one of the two that were put into the chevet of the cathedral in the thirteenth century.

5
Ambulatory

6
Baldachin
It is crowned by a chest that symbolises James the Apostle's tomb.

1

7

➔
Holy Door
Decorated with scenes from the life of Saint James the Greater, the bronze doors are only opened in the Holy Years .

←
James the Knight
The sculpture by Mateo de Prado situated on the baldachin depicts the apostle as the guardian of Christian essence.

4
METRES
is the approximate width of the niche that presides over the high altar of the cathedral.

8

— **Saint Peter's Chapel**

— **Chapel of Mondragón**

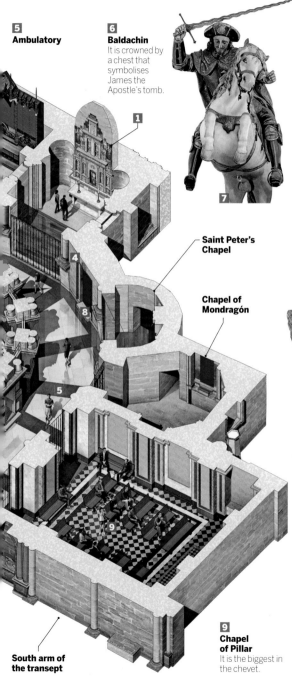

4

8

5

Terracotta angel
Symbol of the sadness at Christ's death, it is part of the altarpiece over the Chapel Mondragón.

Refurbishment attempts

Two complete refurbishment projects were planned for the cathedral but they never came to fruition, the first of which was devised in the mid 13th century, when archbishop Juan Arias designed an apse that was to take up the area of Quintana Square with similar dimensions to that of the central section and the crossing. The other renovation plan was proposed in the 18th century by Archbishop Sebastián de Malvar, who commissioned the construction of a new Holy Door which was never undertaken due to the prelate's death.

9

South arm of the transept

9
Chapel of Pillar
It is the biggest in the chevet.

DESIGN. THE MEDIEVAL STRUCTURE

Altered by successive refurbishments, the original chevet had 5 chapels —a central one and 4 lateral ones— which provided the temple with a balanced ground plan.

Romanesque chevet

Present chevet

The high altar

The visual and spiritual centre of the cathedral, the high altar was planned as a spectacular ornamental arrangement in order to reflect the glory of Saint James.

Baroque landmark

With the aim of highlighting the importance of James the Apostle's tomb, in the mid seventeenth century a complete remodeling of the high altar was planned by Canon José Vega y Verdugo. The work –which was carried out in different phases and counted on the economic support of the Crown– involved the substitution of the medieval altar for a luxurious niche covered by a large baldachin. A Spanish Baroque masterpiece, the ensemble revitalized the interior of the cathedral by means of its imposing pyramidal structure and detailed ornamentation that set the scene for the exaltation of Saint James.

Monumentality
Devised like a great temple, the high altar altered the interior of the Romanesque cathedral.

1 James sitting
The polychrome stone sculpture was carried out by the workshop of Master Mateo.

James the Pilgrim
In 1669 sculptor Pedro del Valle carried out the figure crowning the niche.

Staff

1658

IS THE YEAR
work started on the niche that presides over the high altar of the cathedral.

Plant-life details
The craftsmanship of the silver frontage transmits great vitality and dynamism.

4.6

METRES
high measure the Solomonic columns that form part of the structure of the high altar.

Royal coat of arms
It is over the baldachin to symbolise the identification of the Spanish monarchy with Jacobean cult.

51

LAMPS
illuminated the high altar before they were pillaged in the nineteenth century.

FURNITURE

The pulpits

Built in bronze by craftsman Juan Bautista Celma between 1580 and 1584, the two platforms destined for prayer flank the high altar.

Symbolism. The pulpits include reliefs that reproduce the most significant scenes from the life of Saint James.

➔

The moving of St James' body
A relief situated on the left pulpit recalls the arrival of the body of St James to the Galician coast.

➔

Mythological figures
The bases of the pulpits are supported by beings such as witches and satyrs, symbolising the triumph of good over evil.

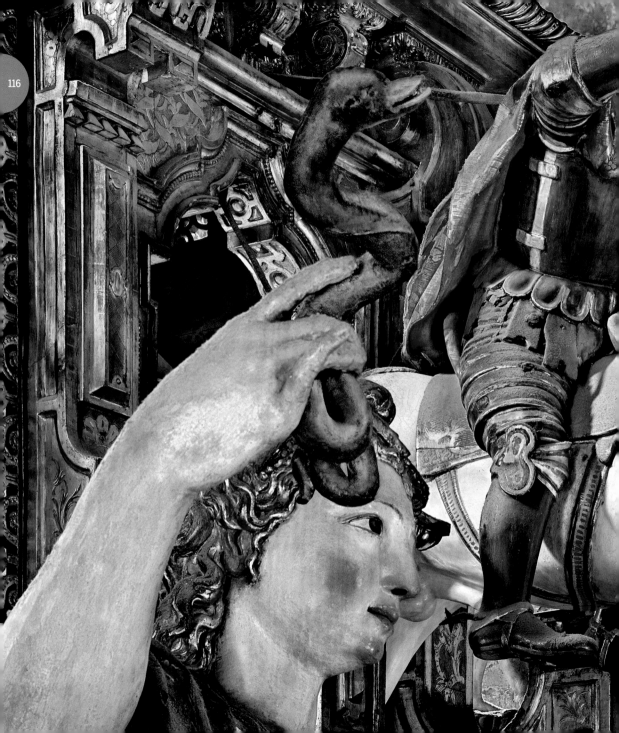

A stage for devotion

The main function of the high altar's decoration is the exaltation of James the Apostle, represented in the camarín and the baldachin in his guise as pilgrim, Patron Saint of Spain and soldier of Jesus Christ.

Cardinal virtues
On each one of the four corners of the baldachin are large polychromed sculptures that symbolise prudence, justice, strength and temperance.

Three images

The high altar's design fulfils the aim to strengthen Jacobean fervour by means of multiple representations of Saint James. The most striking depiction is the one that presides over the *camarín* (a shrine or chamber), recalling the medieval origin of the cathedral and the presence of the tomb, and is accessible from the ambulatory via a staircase which the worshippers climb to carry out the rite of the embrace of the Apostle, the peak of the pilgrimage. Over the niche is a second representation of James, surrounded by four kings that pay tribute to him, staging the unconditional support of the monarchy for the Jacobean cult. Lastly, on the baldachin is a sculpture of James the Apostle on horseback attacking Muslim warriors, symbolising the defence of Christianity.

Pilgrim's staff

1665
IS THE YEAR
architect Domingo de Andrade starts working on the baldachin.

Dynamism
The decoration of the altar conveys a feeling of movement.

James
His attire includes a cape, a garment traditionally associated to pilgrims.

Stairs leading to the *camarín*

Columns of the baldachin

Interior of the *camarín*

Portuguese jasper

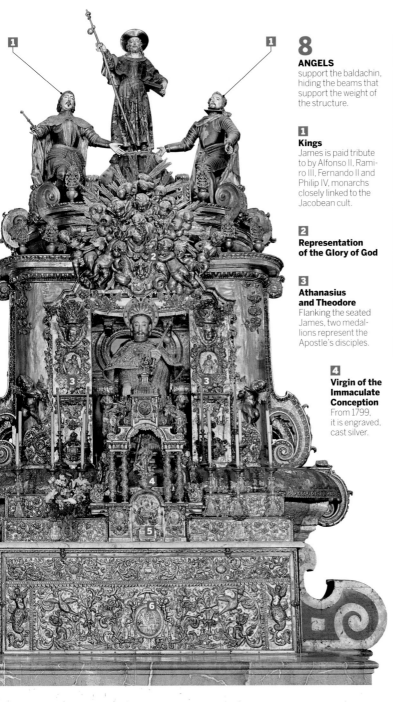

8
ANGELS
support the baldachin, hiding the beams that support the weight of the structure.

1
Kings
James is paid tribute to by Alfonso II, Ramiro III, Fernando II and Philip IV, monarchs closely linked to the Jacobean cult.

2
Representation of the Glory of God

3
Athanasius and Theodore
Flanking the seated James, two medallions represent the Apostle's disciples.

4
Virgin of the Immaculate Conception
From 1799, it is engraved, cast silver.

The angels support the baldachin

Allegory of the cardinal virtues

The Italian influence
Owing to his stays in the Vatican, the Canon that planned the renovation of the high altar, José Vega y Verdugo, was very familiar with the work of Gian Lorenzo Bernini, whose interventions on the Saint Peter's basilica served as a source of inspiration for the design of elements such as the cathedral's baldachin.

5
Tabernacle
Its door is decorated with a relief from the Last Supper.

6
Coat of arms
It is Archbishop Monroy's, who financed the altar's silver.

The apostolic crypt

Renovated in the late nineteenth century to facilitate worshipper access, the tomb situated below the high altar is presided by a silver urn with the relics of James the Apostle and his disciples.

Historicist style
Manufactured by the silversmiths Rey y Martínez, based on the drawings of José Losada, the urn that contains the relics has reliefs of Roman-Byzantine inspiration.

Area of worship

Below the high altar, the burial chamber of Roman origin that conserved the remains of James the Greater and his disciples recuperated its centrality in the cathedral from 1875, when Archbishop Miguel Payá y Rico ordered the reopening of the area (closed since the twelfth century) in order to look for the relics, hidden in the sixteenth century to avoid possible robbery from the English corsair Francis Drake. Four years later, canons Antonio López Ferreiro and José Labín Cabello found bones, whose authenticity was certified by the Vatican , and the crypt was refurbished in Historicist style to aid worship. A marble altar was constructed between the walls conserved from the Roman mausoleum and a silver urn was placed on it. Inside it, a wooden box holds the Apostle's bones with the two saints that brought his body to Galicia.

2.65
METRES
deep is the crypt where James the Apostle's tomb is found.

Plant-life detail
The reliefs on the marble altar over which the urn is deposited are of Paleo-Christian style.

Pantocrator
The figure of Jesus Christ blessing, which decorates the urn, is flanked by the figures of the apostles.

HISTORY. THE DISCOVERER OF THE RELICS

Author of around fifty books, including three historical novels, Antonio López Ferreiro was named in 1871 Canon of the Cathedral of Santiago, where he worked as secretary, relic-keeper and archiver.

The chronicler of the cathedral
Between 1898 and 1910 López Ferreiro published 11 volumes that explored the history of Santiago's temple.

HISTORIA
DE LA
SANTA A. M. IGLESIA DE SANTIAGO
DE COMPOSTELA

1884
IS THE YEAR
in which Pope León XIII certified the authenticity of the relics found five years previously by López Ferreiro.

The ambulatory

Connected to the apsidiole chapels, the nave that circumnavigates the cathedral's high altar guarantees easy passage in order that the pilgrims can gain access to the relics of James the Apostle.

Capitals
The columns that are found at the side of the apsidiole chapels show figures of Romanesque style that represent angels and men wrapped in foliage.

Transit zone

Comprised of a nave that goes round the perimeter of the high altar, the ambulatory constitutes one of the most distinctive architectonic elements of the cathedral, underlining the far-reaching influence of the pilgrimage phenomenon in the design of the temple. Its origin is due to the need to provide a solution to the incessant flow of believers that wanted to worship the apostle's relics, in such a way that this zone was provided with a spaciousness similar to that of the lateral naves in order to channel the movement of the pilgrims in an efficient way but without the interruption of liturgical ceremonies carried out at the altar.

Central stretch of the ambulatory
Built in the framework of the first construction stage of the cathedral, it is covered with groin vaults.

Birds on a capital
A medieval representation of the need to distance oneself from the earthly world and to climb to heaven.

3.85
METRES
is the approximate width of the ambulatory, which has an interior perimeter of 40.7 metres.

Retrochoir
On the jasper and marble base solomonic columns are erected that form part of the Baroque ornamentation of the high altar.

1
Cross
It is over the entrance of the Chapel of Our Lady the White One.

2
Covering
The solomonic columns hide the pillars that support the vaults.

→
Star
It signals the location of the tomb that contains the relics of James the Apostle.

1933
IS THE YEAR
the door of the *Vía Sacra* of the ambulatory is reopened, which was blocked since the C16th.

Floral decoration
The vaults on the ambulatory's central stretch have flower-shape keystones installed in the altar's Baroque renovation.

Connecting function

Apart from facilitating pilgrim access to the relics of James the Apostle, the ambulatory also manages to articulate the communication of the apsidiole chapels, which multiply the spaces of the chevet created for prayer and the expiation of sins. At the same time, the ambulatory interacted with the exterior of the cathedral by means of various minor doors, out of which only the *Vía Sacra* one has been conserved –so-called for the street it connected with–, located between the Chapels of Saint Faith and Saint John.

DECORATION. SOLOMONIC COLUMNS

→
Vines
The decoration of the columns that mark out the perimeter of the high altar refer to the vine, symbol of Jesus Christ's blood.

1669
IS THE YEAR
decorative cladding commenced on the columns that go around the high altar via the ambulatory.

The Holy Door

Located between the Chapel of the Saviour and Saint Peter's Chapel, the entrance used in the holy years is decorated with two large bronze doors that depict the most important scenes during the life of James the Apostle.

Acanthus leaves
Fitting in with the decoration of many of the capitals, the bases of the two columns that flank the Holy Door are decorated with patterns taken from plant-life.

Symbolic entrance

Connected by means of a corridor with the façade that is situated on the façade of Quintana Square and located just a few metres away from the high altar, the Holy Door is only open in the Holy Years, when it then converts into a symbolic entrance way that represents the passage from sin to divine grace. Crowned by a cross of consecration, the door is flanked by two holy water fonts and the sculptures of the prophet Ezequiel and the apostle Judas Thaddeus, proceding from the stone chorus of master builder Mateo. Its bronze doors–designed in 2003 by the artist Suso León– show on its outer face reliefs of Jesus Christ, James and well-known pilgrims, while on the interior there are six important excerpts from the Apostle's life, reinforcing in this manner the role of the chevet as the main space of Jacobean cult.

Stained glass
Manufactured in the year 1896 in eclectic style it shows James the Apostle in a blessing attitude.

Inscription
Over the door, it says the cathedral "is God's house and the door to Paradise".

600
KILOS
weigh the bronze double doors of the Holy Door, which were hung to commemorate the Holy Year of 2004.

Jesus and the Apostles

James praying

James' martyrdom

Transfer of body

Discovery of tomb

28

SEPVLCRVM
EIVS QVASI
GLORIOSVM

The chevet's chapels

Spaces dedicated to the worship of saints and the interment of prominent individuals, the oratories situated in the cathedral's apse are presided over by striking altarpieces and ornamental elements of diverse styles.

↩
Virgin of Montserrat
This copy of the Romanesque carving worshipped in the Monastery of Montserrat (Barcelona), is in the Chapel of Our Lady the White One.

Original and renovated oratories
The oldest of the chevet's seven chapels is the Saviour one, which was the starting point of the construction of the cathedral and which has a 16th century stone altarpiece. The other chapels that have a medieval stamp are the Saint Faith –with a Renaissance altarpiece designed by Casas Novoa, author of the Obradoiro Façade–, whilst the Saint John one, also of Romanesque origin, had its Romanesque layout altered in the 16th and 17th centuries, when it was enlarged with Baroque decoration. Between this last chapel and that of the Chapel of the Saviour is Our Lady the White One, built in the 15th century and decorated with a neo-Gothic altar. The Chapel of Mondragón dates back to the 16th century, which has Gothic details such as its terracotta altarpiece; while the Pilar Chapel was completed in 1723 with a detailed Baroque style design.

**120
SQUARE METRES**
is the rough surface area that the Chapel of Pilar occupies.

Altarpiece from the Chapel of Pilar
Designed by Casas Novoa in marble and jasper, it is decorated with angels.

↩
Chapel of the Saviour
In the central part of the chevet, it has a C16th altarpiece.

Chapel of Mondragón

Saint Peter's Chapel

Saint John's Chapel

Saint Bartholomew's Chapel

07 | THE DISSEMINATION OF HERITAGE
The Cathedral Museum

Diverse exhibition spaces hold works of great historical value that highlight the splendour of the temple.

With the aim to bring worshippers closer to the Gospel while, at the same time, to embellish the areas used for worship, right from the outset the Catholic Church enthusiastically promoted the creation of works of art and monopolised cultural activity in periods such as the Middle Ages. This function as sponsor meant that it amassed a wealth of cultural heritage, preserved not only for its artistic and historic worth, but also for the fact that it was proof of the spirituality of the community of worshippers. In the nineteenth century the need was recognised to organise this legacy under museum criteria which would highlight the contextual importance of the works and facilitate historical investigation, coinciding with the creation of large public museums and the rise of archeology. In the case of the Cathedral of Santiago de Compostela –which as well as holding a large variety of liturgical objects in disuse was also recipient of numerous pilgrim offerings–, the formulation of the first proposals to exhibit part of its artistic collection in a permanent way led to the foundation of the present Cathedral Museum, the institution commissioned with conserving and disseminating the patrimony of a temple that since its very beginnings has been one of the great cultural centres of Christian Europe.

The cloister
Apart from acting as an area of communication between different parts of the cathedral, it symbolises celestial paradise and the purity of the Virgin.

Gothic art
The Cathedral Museum holds priceless exhibits of sculpture developed in the Iberian Peninsula between the C13th and C15th.

The heart of the museum

The cathedral's collections are concentrated in the cloister, an area built in the sixteenth century with the collaboration of diverse architects, who fused Gothic elements with Renaissance style decorative details.

Distribution by levels

With the crypt of the Glory Portico, the Gelmírez Palace and the roofs as complementary spaces, most of the collection of the Cathedral Museum is exhibited on the four floors of the western wing of the cloister, an area or quadrangular layout designed to accommodate the clerics that participated in the governance of the diocese. On display on the two lower floors are the archeological remains that provide an insight into the origins of the cathedral, while the two upper floors –where the library and the Chapterhouse are– are dedicated to the collections of goldwork, textilework and painting. The Treasury and the Chapel of Relics, situated on the northern stretch of the cloister ensemble, are also within the museum area and delve deeply into the architectonic singularity of the cathedral and its priceless artistic content.

✳ A monumental courtyard

The cloister of the Cathedral of Santiago is one of the largest in the Iberian Peninsula.

Chapel of Alba

Founded in 1529, it is presided over by an C18th altarpiece that depicts the transfiguration of Christ.

2 Treasury

Within the cloister chapel dedicated to Saint Fernando, it holds an important collection of gold work.

Cresting

The cloister is finished off on its upper part with a typical coronation of Plateresque style.

Chapel of Relics

Façade of Obradoiro Square

3 Library

With a vault decorated with scenes from James' life, it holds a rich book collection on its shelves.

4 Paving

It has tombstones of the monks buried in the cloister, thus showing the funeral function of the area.

5 Cloister façade of Rúa de Fonseca

6
Termination of Treasury Tower

7
Watch Tower

35
METRES
is the length of each one of the wings of the cloister, whose width is 5.80 metres.

1590
IS THE YEAR
in which construction on the cloister finishes, 69 years after it had been started.

Fountain. Of Romanesque style, it was originally in the Door of Paradise.

Treasury façade

6

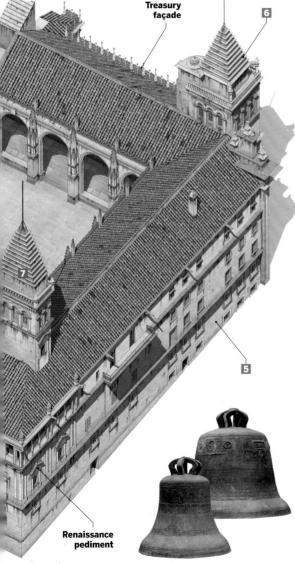

7

5

Renaissance pediment

8
Chapterhouse
Devised as the meeting space of the canons, it is presided by an altar with the figure of Saint James.

Starred vault
Keystones decorated with varied reliefs terminate the roofs of the cloister.

The cloister area
Started in 1521 by order of Archbishop Alonso III of Vilaseca, the construction of the cloister –designed over a gallery damaged in the 15th century by a series of popular uprisings– fell upon architect Juan de Álava, in order to later pass through the hands of Rodrigo Gil de Hontañón, Juan de Herrera and Gaspar de Arce. Despite this shared authorship, the area conserves great unity in its four wings, structured around wide arcades and covered with starred vaults that blend in with the medieval origin of the building.

1510
IS THE YEAR
Juan de Álava presents the work program, which would start 11 years later.

Bells
In the cloister are the bells that originate from the Clocktower, the largest of which is called the Berenguela, from the 18th century.

8

A legacy of incalculable value

The permanent collection of the museum offers a complete tour around the cathedral's past by means of pieces from different periods, many of them originating from archeological excavations or offerings to Saint James.

 The Epiphany
Virgin and Child protagonise the 14th century tympanum of the Lady Leonor Chapel, now gone.

2 **Personages**
Saint Joseph and the patron of the chapel, Lady Leonor.

Numerous origins

The Cathedral Museum divides its collection into two large areas. On one side, it gathers architectonic and decorative elements that, owing to the successive remodellings carried out in the temple over the centuries, were taken from their original position, such as the case of the reconstruction of the stone chorus of master builder Mateo or some sculptures coming from the former Paradise and Platerías façades. On the other side, there are also the art collections, which include priceless works which were donations or offerings, such as altarpieces, reliefs, sculptures, paintings, gold work and tapestries.

⊘ The Adoration of the Magi
Known as the tympanum of Lady Leonor, it was found in a chapel on the west side,

Natural decoration
Amongst the pieces exhibited are archeological remains from the old city of Compostela.

1928
IS THE YEAR
the museum was founded, on the initiative of Canon Robustiano Sande.

The Magi
They bring gifts to baby Jesus.

⊖ Horses from Procession of the Magi
Relief from the retrochoir façade.

⊘ Stone chorus
The museum has a partial reconstruction with original pieces.

The Virgin holds Jesus on her throne

3
The angel censers
Two angels scatter incense with botafumeiros over Jesus Christ and Mary.

Saint Michael
A polychromed granite sculpture crowned one of the towers of the disappeared north façade of Saint James Cathedral, now the Azabachería.

12
TAPESTRIES
based on sketches carried out by Francisco de Goya are on display in the Cathedral Museum's rooms.

Month of February
The Paradise Façade has reliefs which depict the months of the year in an allegorical manner.

4
Adam and Eve
It is a relief from the missing Paradise Façade.

5
James in Hispania
Wooden relief put into position in the C16th into the stone chorus.

DECORATIVE ARTS
Tapestries
On the upper floor of the cloister some of the tapestries from the cathedral are on display, amongst which are works by Goya, Rubens and Teniers.

'The Buen Retiro Garden'. Its creator, José del Castillo, is considered one of the masters of tapestry of the 19th century.

'The Majo with a guitar'
It is one of the sketches that Goya carried out for the Royal Factory of Tapestries of Madrid.

'Life of Achiles'. The museum conserves four pieces from this series based on sketches created by Rubens.

Altarpiece with scenes from the life of James. On the occasion of his pilgrimage to Santiago de Compostela in 1456, John Goodyear, parish priest of Chal, on the Isle of Wight (United Kingdom), offered this altarpiece that is on display in the Cathedral Museum. Comprised of five polychrome alabaster panels mounted on wood, the piece shows in chronological order some of the most striking episodes of the apostle's life, starting with his first meeting with Jesus Christ at Lake Tiberias and finishing with the moving of his body to the Iberian Peninsula.

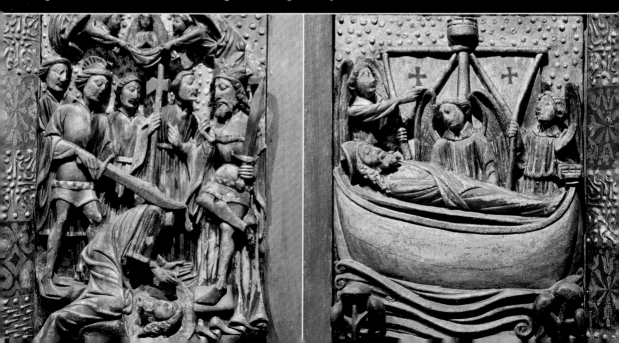

The Chapel of the Relics

Located in the north wing of the cloistral arrangement, the vaulted room that holds the sepulchres of the diverse kings buried in the cathedral displays a large collection of relics accumulated since medieval times.

Reliquary of Saint Pauline
Created by goldsmith Jorge Cedeira in 1553, this bust exhibited on the altarpiece of the chapel contains the skull of a saint originating from Germany.

Diverse functions

Covered by a tracery vault with Burgos Gothic influence and designed by architect Juan de Álava, the space that guards the relics of Santiago Cathedral owes its spaciousness to its origin as a chapterhouse. From 1535 the room combined its initial purpose with that of mausoleum, by becoming the main place to receive the kings' sepulchres which up until that time had been found in other parts of the cathedral; while in 1633 it took on the function of reliquary, with the construction of a large altarpiece – replaced by another of neo-Gothic style in the twentieth century following a fire– where the remains of saints can be found originating from all over the world. The chapel was thus converted into one of the most important spaces of the cloister, highlighting the symbolism of the cathedral by means of the exhibition of its holy patrimony.

1921

IS THE YEAR
in which a fire destroys the original altarpiece of the Chapel of the Relics.

Royal pantheon
The Chapel of the Relics holds the tombs of León monarchs Alfonso IX and Fernando II.

Altarpiece
Carved in cedar wood in 1924 by Maximino Magariños, it was donated by Galicians emigrated to Cuba.

TREASURE. THE GOLD COLLECTION

The room dedicated to the cathedral treasure –which is also called the Chapel of Saint Fernando– brings together valuable works of gold carried out between the 11th and 20th centuries, from pieces directly related to liturgy to objects donated by pilgrims to the cathedral.

Ciborium of Monroy

James Moor-Slayer

Crucifix of Ordoño II

Monstrance

Library and chapterhouse

The rooms on the west wing of the cloister stand out for their book collections and tapestries and their Baroque design, designed by Lucas Ferro Caaveiro in the mid-eighteenth century following a fire that destroyed the original rooms.

← **Pulpit**
Situated in the library, it was manufactured by Francisco de Lens in the C18th.

→ **'Codex Calixtinus'**
In the library there is a facsimile volume from 1993 on display.

01